LOCOMOTIVES

in detail

STANIER 4-6-0   **2**   **CLASS 5**

LOCOMOTIVES
in detail
2

STANIER 4-6-0   **CLASS 5**

JOHN JENNISON & DAVID CLARKE

Ian Allan
PUBLISHING

The genesis of this book goes back over 10 years when we were carrying out research on the LMS 4-6-0 Class 5 for the second of our Brassmasters 4mm scale model locomotive kits. Here we must acknowledge the part played by our customers; they want to know what a particular engine looked like at a specific date, which type of tender it was paired with and the style of livery it carried. One well-known writer and modeller said that, 'of course, the kit will allow me to build one of the first 10 of the class as running in Scotland in late 1934'. At this point it became apparent that some serious research was needed to make sure that as far as possible we covered all of the variants as they evolved over the thirty plus years the class was in service. This resulted in many hours poring over drawings and examining the official Engine History Cards, but we were soon to discover that they told only part of the story. The other route we have taken is to use photographs both to confirm what the drawings and History Cards told us, but also to identify further visual variants on which these were silent.

Over the years we have probably read every book and article which has mentioned the class; some of these have been very helpful whilst others have been potentially misleading. We ourselves have been closely involved in the recent and forthcoming books from Wild Swan on the Class 5, and hope that this volume is complementary to those publications, especially as far as the photographic content is concerned. For those wanting more information, particularly on mechanical details and background, we recommend the following books:

LMS Locomotive Profiles 5. The Mixed Traffic Class 5s 5000 to 5224 - Hunt/James/Essery/Jennison/Clarke - Wild Swan 2003 - ISBN 1 874103 87 9.
Pictorial Supplement to LMS Locomotive Profile 5 - Jennison/Clarke/Hunt/James/Essery - Wild Swan 2003 - ISBN 1 874103 83 6.
Stanier 4-6-0s at Work - A. J. Powell – Ian Allan Limited 1983 - ISBN 071101342 X.
Living with London Midland Locomotives – A. J. Powell – Ian Allan 1977 – ISBN 0711007284.
Stanier Locomotive Classes – A. J. Powell – Ian Allan 1991 - ISBN 0 7110 1962 2.
The Stanier 4-6-0s Of The LMS – J. W. P. Rowledge and B. Reed – David & Charles 1977 – ISBN 0 7153 7385 4.
Raising Steam on the LMS - A. F. Cook RCTS 1999 – ISBN 0 901115 85 1.

When we chose the Class 5 to model we knew that it was going to be a major task to ensure we identified all of the visual differences so that we could incorporate these in our kit. We even talked about producing a guide to the class so that modellers would have all of the information needed to produce an accurate model of a particular locomotive, especially to highlight the areas of visual difference. We apologise that it has taken so long to produce our 'Modeller's Guide', but we hope that we have finally produced a book which meets our original aim.

John Jennison & David Clarke
July 2004

Series Created & Edited by Jasper Spencer-Smith.
Design and artwork: Nigel Pell.
Produced by JSS Publishing Limited,
Bournemouth, Dorset, England.

Title spread: Class 5 No 44795 on the Settle–Carlisle line at Ais Gill with an up freight, a classic train for a mixed traffic locomotive, May 1956. (CR/EC)

First published 2004

ISBN 0 7110 3014 6

Published by Ian Allan Publishing

an imprint of Ian Allan Publishing Ltd, Hersham, Surrey, KT12 4RG.

Printed by Ian Allan Printing Ltd, Hersham, Surrey, KT12 4RG.

Code: 0409/A2

Photograph Credits
Colour-Rail (CR) and their photographers
A. E. R. Cope (EC); A Sainty Collection (AS);
K. Cooper (KC); M. Chapman (MC); A. Dow (DOW);
T. J. Edgington (TJE); K. M. Falconer (KMF); F. Hornby (FH); G. H. Hunt (GHH); N. Harrop (NH); P. J. Hughes (PH); P. Hutchinson (PHu); M. A. Kirby (MAK);
J. B. McCann (JMc); T. B. Owen (TO); Historic Model Railway Society (HMR); S. M. Watkins (SW).
Also Colin P. Boocock (CPB); B. Green (BG); R. J. Henley (RJH); Ian Allan Library (IAL); Gavin Morrison (GM);
P Ransome-Wallis (PRW)
Via authors' collection (AC).

INTRODUCTION

'All "Black 5s" were the same' say many enthusiasts.
In fact there were a number of variations, both in mechanical
configuration and the many versions of 'standard' liveries.

The LMS 4-6-0 Class 5 introduced by W. A. Stanier in 1934 is one of the classic British steam locomotives of all time. The Class 5 worked all over the London, Midland & Scottish (LMS) system, from Bristol and Bournemouth in the south to the far north of Scotland, remained in service until the final day of British Railways (BR) steam, and worked

Left:
No 45308 on an express train at Manchester Victoria Station. (CR/NH)

almost every type of train. The sheer number of locomotives in the class (842) was testimony to their effectiveness, and they were built over 17 years by three railway workshops and two private builders. As subsequent batches were introduced they incorporated improvements and modifications to boilers, motion, frames, tenders, wheels and fittings; these were sometimes applied to locomotives from previous batches (and sometimes taken off again!!) We have found over 100 officially recorded modifications, some applied to a handful of locomotives and others to the whole class and to complicate matters further, normal works procedures resulted in exchanges of tenders and boilers (and later) even main frames.

The aim of this book is to guide the modeller through the complexities of the Class 5s, pointing out the variations between batches over time in service. It is not, and does not attempt to be, a detailed history of the class and

nor, in the space at our disposal, are we able to explain other than in outline why the design evolved over the years. Where possible, we have used photographs to illustrate the points made in the text and have provided extended captions to add further detail.

The principal visual differences were in the boilers, cabs, tenders, motion and valve gear. Changes in design arose as a result of experience in service and in response to changing operating conditions after World War Two. We hope that this guide will enable readers to identify from a dated photograph the correct combination of features on any particular locomotive at any time in service. We have produced a table to summarise the as-built configuration and allow easy reference, and the text describes subsequent changes. The photographs we have selected have been chosen to show as many of the possible variations on engines and tenders in the class.

Far left:
No 45225, the first Long Firebox Armstrong Whitworth engine working in as built condition in the 1950s. (AC)

A number of different terms have been used in previous books and articles on the class, some of which differ from those used in official railway documents and drawings. Indeed, the class was commonly known among enthusiasts as the 'Black 5' rather than the Class 5. We have, with one exception, used official terminology so that the text is unambiguous. The only place where we believe it is clearer for the current purpose to use an alternative is for the type of boiler and firebox. The LMS employed the term Vertical Throatplate for the earlier design of boilers and Straight Throatplate for the later type. We have adopted Short Firebox for the former and Long Firebox for the latter on the grounds that these are better descriptions of this key visual difference. Where we refer to the left or right-hand side of the locomotive this is when looking forward from the cab.

CONSTRUCTION & MODIFICATIONS

The Class 5 locomotives were built in batches of varying numbers over many years, and whilst there was generally uniformity within each batch as built, variations emerged as soon as the locomotives visited the workshops. The size of the class and the repair procedures used at the workshops meant that tenders and even major components such as boilers and frames were exchanged as a matter of course, so that the configuration of any individual locomotive often changed at every major overhaul. The 'worst offender' was St. Rollox, which appears to have created almost every possible combination

of boiler/firebox, fittings and livery. Some individual locomotives provide a trap for the unwary, two of the best examples being No 5082 and No 5087 which over the years carried all four different variants of boiler. Therefore when modelling one of the class, it is particularly important to have a dated photograph of the specific prototype locomotive.

VISUAL DIFFERENCES

We have summarised the main visual differences in the class as built in the table opposite. Further variants are dealt with in each section under the appropriate heading. Unfortunately, we do not have space here to describe the many 'unseen' differences and modifications, nor in other than in the broadest terms to discuss the reasons for the design changes. For those who want this detail we would refer you to the *LMS Locomotive Profiles* on the Class 5s of which the authors of this book are co-authors.

When using the table it is important to note that the locomotives are listed in the order of the batches in which they were built. Numbers were allocated to each batch, and therefore individual engines did not always appear in the order implied by the running numbers. Where there was simultaneous construction by more than one works, they are ordered by which batch was started first. When the text states that a configuration was applied from a particular engine number onwards, this refers to the order in the table and not the simple numerical order.

STANIER 4-6-0 CLASS 5 CHRONOLOGY

Engine Nos	Date built	Engine Nos	Date built
5020–69	1934–5	4768–82	1947
5000–19	1935	4758–64	1947
5070–4	1935	4765–7	1947
5075–124	1935	44738–47	1948
5125–224	1935	44748–57	1948
5225–451	1936–7	44698–717	1948
5452–71	1938	44718–27	1949
5472–99	1943–4	44728–37	1949
4800–25	1944	44658–67	1949
4826–60	1944	44668–77	1950
4861–920	1945	44678–85	1950
4921–31; 4967–81	1946	44688–97	1950
4932–66; 4982–96	1945–7	44686–7	1951
4997–9; 4783–99	1947		

STANIER 4-6-0 CLASS 5 CONSTRUCTION DETAILS

From	To	Built	Boiler	Cab	Motion	Tender
5020	5069	Vulcan Foundry	Short Firebox domeless No domed covers on firebox		27ft2in wheelbase Plain coupling rods 11ft3in connecting rods Cranked/flat combination lever	Riveted tanks
5000	5019	Crewe				
5075	5124	Vulcan Foundry	Short Firebox domeless	Sliding windows	27ft2in wheelbase Plain coupling rods 11ft3in connecting rods Straight/fluted combination lever	
5070	5074	Crewe				
5125	5224	Armstrong Whitworth				
5225	5451	Armstrong Whitworth				Welded tanks
5452	5471	Crewe		Sliding windows Handrail stanchions		
5472	5499	Derby	Long Firebox domed Top Feed on second barrel ring			
4800	4806	Derby				
4807	4825	Derby				
4826	4911	Crewe				
4932	4950*	Horwich				
4912	4931	Crewe			27ft2in wheelbase Fluted coupling rods 10ft10in connecting rods Straight/fluted combination lever	
4951	4996	Horwich				
4967	4981	Crewe				
4982	4966**					
4997*	4999	Horwich	Long Firebox domed Top Feed on first barrel ring	Fixed windows Handrail stanchions		Part welded tanks
4783*	4799	Horwich				
4768	4782	Crewe				
4758	4766	Crewe	Long Firebox domed Top Feed on first barrel ring Extended smokebox		27ft6in wheelbase Fluted coupling rods 10ft10in connecting rods Straight/fluted combination lever	
4698	4717	Horwich				
4718	4737	Crewe				
4658	4667	Crewe				
4668	4697**	Horwich				

From	To	Built	Boiler	Cab	Motion	Tender
4767		Crewe	Long Firebox domed Top Feed on first barrel ring Extended smokebox	Fixed windows Handrail stanchions	27ft6in wheelbase Fluted coupling rods 10ft10in connecting rods Stephenson valve gear	Part welded tanks
4748	4757	Crewe		Cut-off at platform level	27ft6in wheelbase Fluted coupling rods 10ft10in connecting rods Caprotti valve gear	
4738	4747	Crewe		Cut-off below platform level		
4686	4687	Horwich				

* Engines No 4783 and No 4997 were planned to have boilers with the top feed on the first barrel ring but actually received second barrel ring boilers.

** Engines Nos 4965 and 4966 and Nos 4696 and 4697 were built with coal-weighing tenders.

CHAPTER ONE

BOILERS

The boilers were based on contemporary GWR practice.
The design was then developed and fitted with
higher superheating. After World War Two, new features
were incorporated to reduce maintenance costs.

The first engines were built soon after W.A. Stanier joined the LMS from the Great Western Railway (GWR) and, like the contemporary 'Jubilee' and 'Princess' classes, incorporated many GWR features which Stanier had brought from his time at Swindon. One of the most important was the tapered boiler and Belpaire firebox, which initially had the same low level of superheating as used on the GWR. It soon became apparent that different operating conditions on the LMS, particularly the type of coal used, caused steaming problems with Stanier's new designs resulting in poor coal consumption compared with their predecessors. Although this was more marked with the 'Jubilee' than the Class 5s, there were numerous experiments with draughting and superheating which resulted in a rapid redesign of the boilers for both classes in early 1936.

MAIN VARIANTS

Visually, the firebox was lengthened by 12in and the boiler shortened by a corresponding amount. A separate dome and topfeed was provided, compared with the first Short Firebox design which had a combined dome and topfeed (commonly referred to as 'domeless'). Once the Long Firebox design was finalised, all new boilers including spares

were built to that design. This meant that 13 of the original Short Firebox engines were given Long Firebox boilers in 1936/7 to create a spares pool for the Short Firebox boilers without having to build any new boilers to the old design.

The picture became even more complex when 57 of the original domeless Short Firebox boilers were rebuilt with separate domes and increased superheating between 1937 and 1940. The story did not stop there, because the routine exchange of boilers during heavy overhauls resulted in changes not only between the variants of Short Firebox boilers, but also with the Long Firebox boilers. We have identified over 30 locomotives in the Nos 5000 to 5224 series which at some point carried Long Firebox boilers, and three examples (Nos 5433, 5443, 5461) of Long Firebox engines which ran with Short Firebox boilers.

The visual differences increased after the war: the pre-war Long Firebox boilers had the topfeed on the second ring of the boiler close to the dome, but from early 1947 all-new boiler construction was to a modified design with the top feed on the first ring of the boiler barrel. As with the early boilers, normal works visits resulted in locomotives built with forward top feed boilers being fitted with the

Left:
No 5024 in the 1930s as built with tall chimney, domeless boiler, external top feedpipes, no steam heat pipes, crosshead vacuum pump and riveted tender. Note the large hole in the front bogie axle. (AC)

Below:
No 45190 at Shrewsbury shed (ex-LMS side) with a welded tender. It has a domeless boiler as built. Note the door lug on the smokebox and also over-head power warning flashes. The tender carries a late-style BR totem. (AC)

Above:
No 5026 as built with a riveted tender, Short Firebox domeless boiler, external topfeed pipes, and no platform under the smokebox. The requirement for a platform soon became evident and those locomotives delivered without were very quickly so fitted. (AC)

Right:
No 5013 in as built condition, September 1937. It is fitted with a Short Firebox domeless boiler, steam heat pipes, crosshead vacuum pump, riveted tender, and tablet exchange apparatus. (AC)

early pattern of Long Firebox boiler, and vice versa. We know of over 70 changes to, and 50 from, the forward topfeed pattern; we are not aware of any of the longer wheelbase engines ever having Short Firebox boilers.

On a number of engines the separate top feed cover was fitted with the cover intended for the dome, giving the effect of a double-domed engine. This appears to have been confined to repairs at St Rollox works which sent out engines with every possible combination of dome and top feed.

WASHOUT PLUGS AND INSPECTION DOORS

All of the Short Firebox boilers had five washout plugs on each side of the firebox at crown level. On Nos 5010 to 5019 and from No 5070 onwards two washout inspection doors with small domed covers were provided on each side on the top shoulders of the firebox. As boilers were exchanged they could be found on earlier locomotives, or could

Above:
No 5031 in 1936-style livery and converted to Long Firebox boiler. There are no covers on the shoulders of the firebox. Note the large holes on the bogie axles. A BTH speedometer is fitted; this equipment was removed during World War Two, although many engines retained the large bracket below the platform. It is fitted with a riveted tender. (AC)

Left:
No 45214, at Eastfield, Glasgow, 10 April 1954. It has a Short Firebox boiler with separate dome and topfeed. There are no washout plugs on the firebox shoulders. Note the short chimney and lug on the smokebox door. A welded tender is fitted. Note the large cabside numerals (AC)

be absent from those originally fitted; the early boilers were not retro-fitted. The boiler clothing normally stayed with the engine and not the boiler, and therefore some engines had flat covers over the holes in the cladding where the inspection doors would have been fitted.

On the Long Firebox boilers there were five washout plugs on the left-hand side of the firebox and six on the right hand side; the two washout inspection doors and covers were the same as on the later Short Firebox boilers.

SMOKEBOX

The Class 5s had the new LMS standard 'drumhead' smokebox, based on GWR practice, with a cylindrical smokebox resting on a cast saddle.

The smokebox door had a central dart, locking handle and swung on two hinged straps. At the top, the door had a horizontal handrail with the upper lamp bracket attached above.

On Long Firebox locomotives a counter weight was fitted to the left hand-side of the

Right:
View along the top of the Long Firebox boiler of No 45305. Note the cleats behind the dome for the boiler clothing retaining straps. The topfeed has the additional cover introduced by Ivatt.(AC)

smokebox door/ring to help carry the weight of the door. As boilers were changed, these were removed from some locomotives. It could also be seen on Short Firebox engines.

On the post-war longer wheelbase loco-motives the frames were lengthened by 4in to accommodate roller-bearing axleboxes; thus the smokebox had to be extended by 4in to compensate for the boiler being moved back.

Self-cleaning smokeboxes were introduced in 1945 with No 4885; the interior of the smokebox was fitted with wire-mesh screens, the objective of which was to prevent ash settling on the smokebox floor and to avoid cleaning out the smokebox

between boiler wash-outs. The engines fitted carried a cast iron 'SC' plate on the lower half of the smokebox door (the first few had SC painted on the middle of the smokebox door for a short period).From the 1946 Crewe and Horwich batches (beginning with No 4922 and No 4942 respectively), all new locomotives were fitted with rocking grates and hopper ash-pans.This was to speed up disposal by reducing the time required emptying ashpans; the hopper door operating gear was visible between the driving and trailing coup-led wheels on the left-hand side of the locomotive.

During the run down of steam in the 1960s some locomotives had the 'SC' screens removed

Above:
No 5232 in the original condition fitted with a Long Firebox domed boiler and welded tender. Note the large holes in the driving axles. It is finished in 1936-style livery. (AC)

Right:
No 45312 at Edge Hill, Liverpool, in the 1960s. It has the topfeed on the first ring of the boiler barrel. The large cabside numerals indicate that the engine had received an overhaul at Cowlairs. A post-1957 BR totem is on the tender. Automatic Warning System (AWS) is fitted.(AC)

Right:
No 45461 at Carmine, Scotland, in the 1950s. Holes in the bufferbeam indicate where the brackets were fitted when a snowplough was mounted. It has a riveted tender and tablet exchange apparatus. Originally built with a Long Firebox boiler, it is one of only three which were converted to a Short Firebox boiler. The domeless boiler does not have the usual combined dome and topfeed but has a topfeed cover only. This type of topfeed cover on a domeless boiler was a speciality of St Rollox and was seen on a number of Short Firebox engines. (AC)

and the plate removed. One of the Caprotti engines was seen in 1961 with 'Not SC' painted above the shed plate, presumably to remind the enginemen that the smokebox would require emptying each time the engine was disposed.

The rivet patterns on the smokebox changed during the life of the class as routine maintenance and modification were carried out, with the earlier locomotives having more flush rivets than the later versions. The Short Firebox locomotives had flush rivets on the smokebox door ring, but the Long Firebox engines, with the exception of those built at Derby, had snaphead rivets at the bottom of the ring. In later years additional rivets appeared

on the smokebox wrapper plates where inner liner plates were fitted, and boiler and smokebox changes and renewals produced other variations.

LAMP IRONS

The lamp iron above the handrail on the smokebox door was moved for safety reasons when overhead electrification spread in the 1960s, to a position (when viewed from the front of the locomotive) to the right of the central locking handle. The central lamp iron above the bufferbeam was also moved to the right to remain directly beneath the upper lamp iron.

Left:
No 4953 in LMS livery, with the topfeed on the first ring of the boiler (it was originally built with second ring topfeed boiler). A part welded tender with plain axleboxes is fitted.(AC)

Left:
No 4785 as built with topfeed on the first ring of the boiler, is finished in 1946 LMS-style livery. It is fitted to a part welded tender with plain axleboxes. (AC)

CHIMNEY

The first Vulcan Foundry batch (Nos 5020 to 5069) had chimneys which were $2^{1}/_{2}$in taller than those from Crewe (Nos 5000 to 5019), which became standard for all subsequent construction and were fitted to the earlier batch at the first general repair. However, the taller chimneys sometimes reappeared following works visits and at least one, No 5068, retained the tall chimney for some years after being fitted with a domed boiler.

A few of the post-war engines were built with a double chimney: Nos 4765 to 4767 and Caprotti locomotives Nos 4755 to 4757 and Nos 4686 to 4687. Nos 4765 and 4766 were the only two 'standard' Class 5s fitted with the double chimney. No 4765 carried a single chimney for a short time during 1950 and No 4767 had a single chimney from 1953 up to withdrawal from service in September 1967.

STEAM PIPE CASINGS

The first ten Vulcan Foundry locomotives (Nos 5020 to 5029) had a 'scalloped' cut-out at the lower front of the steam pipe casings instead of the very small cut-out on all subsequent construction. Although most of these casings remained with the original locomotives, p.20▶

Right:
No 44794 stands under the up starter signal at Dunblane with the 12.30pm Aberdeen to Glasgow train, May 1966. (CR/PHu)

Below:
No 45151 on a fitted freight leaving Kingmoor Yard, Carlisle, 14 August 1960. The engine has been fitted with a forward topfeed boiler but with the cover from a domeless boiler, thus giving the impression of a 'double-domed' engine. (GM)

Left:
No 44766 with a double chimney and finished in plain black livery at Willesden shed, August 1964. (CR/SW)

Below:
No 45458, a Long Firebox locomotive fitted with a first ring forward topfeed boiler (it was originally built with a second ring type). It is also fitted with AWS equipment. It is in ex-works condition at Polmadie shed, September 1959. (CR/KC)

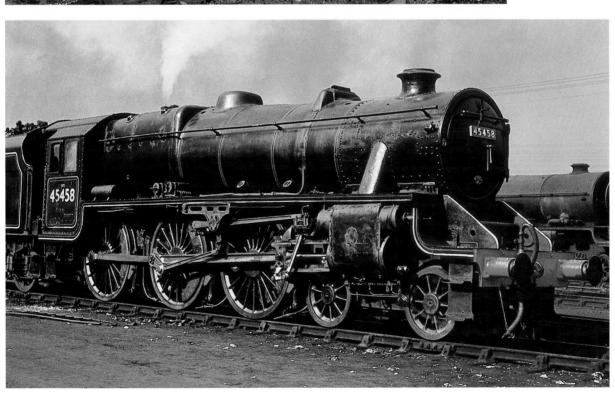

some were fitted on to other class engines following works visits, a set even surviving on No 44871 on the last day of BR steam working in August 1968.

TOP FEED PIPES

All of the class had top feed pipes flush with boiler clothing, except for Nos 5020 to 5069 where the pipes were fitted over the clothing. The latter were altered to flush fitting at the locomotive's first heavy overhaul.

STEAM LANCE EQUIPMENT

Steam lance cocks were positioned low near the base of the right-hand side of the smokebox (looking forward from the cab) on the Short Firebox locomotives; on the Long

Firebox locomotives these were moved to a height just above the top of the steam pipe. As boilers were changed and smokeboxes renewed the position was often reversed from that as built. The internal pipes suffered corrosion problems and in the 1960s many locomotives were fitted with the BR type which was mounted in the low position with a long external steam feed pipe from above the handrail.

INJECTORS

A Davies & Metcalfe Class H exhaust steam injector was fitted under the cab slightly to the right of the centreline of the locomotive. It was the equivalent of a feed water heater combined with an injector as a single unit, and operated on exhaust steam drawn from the blastpipe, assisted

only by a small amount of live steam. The unit had to be fitted between the frames because it was larger and more complex than the live-steam injector and had a large feed pipe from the smokebox. The smaller Gresham & Craven live-steam injector was mounted under the cab on the left-hand side.

EJECTORS

Both large and small vacuum brake ejectors were provided, mounted close to the front of the cab and fitted with a long exhaust pipe to the smokebox on the left-hand side of the boiler. The large ejector created the vacuum quickly but used a large volume of steam to do so; the small ejector was therefore provided for continuous use to maintain the working vacuum after it had been created by the large ejector.

ELECTRIC LIGHTING

Electric lighting was fitted to four post-war locomotives (No 44658 and Nos 4765, 4766 and 4767) with power supplied by a Stone's steam turbo-generating set located on the running plate adjacent to the smokebox on the right-hand side. The equipment, which powered cab lights and head lamps was removed, because of numerous defects in the period 1952/53.

CHAPTER TWO

FRAMES, WHEELS, RUNNING GEAR

*The relatively lightweight frames of the first engines
soon gave problems in service; on later engines
the frames were strengthened and other features
were introduced to improve availability.*

The mechanical differences between batches were less apparent than many of the other variations, and with few exceptions there were no obvious visible changes on individual engines.

FRAMES

In order to save weight, the main frames on the first 451 locomotives were manufactured from high-tensile steel which was only 1in thick; this was subsequently increased to $1^1/_{16}$in thick from No 5452 onwards, and again to $1^1/_8$in from No 4997 (Horwich) and No 4768 (Crewe). Minimal staying was fitted to reduce the weight of the locomotive, but the consequence of this was a major problem with cracking, particularly at the top corners of the horn gaps, and various stiffening stay arrangements were tried. Repair was usually achieved by welding, but in extreme cases patches were welded on.

In 1943 a spare set of frames was constructed at Crewe allowing locomotives which required major frame repairs to be returned more quickly into service. When the first engine requiring a major repair arrived, it was stripped and rebuilt on the new frames, and once the original frames had been repaired these became the spare set. This resulted in many exchanges of frames, both between the Short Firebox and the Long Firebox locomotives,

and between locomotives from different builders.

The frames were lengthened from No 4768 onwards because the wheelbase was increased by 4in to accommodate the roller bearings fitted experimentally to 20 of the class; to simplify marking out, all engines built thereafter had the longer wheelbase even when plain-bearing axleboxes were fitted.

The builder's plates were usually permanently mounted on the frames, so engines built at Crewe or Vulcan Foundry appeared with Armstrong Whitworth plates, and vice versa. In some cases engines were outshopped with two different makers' plates, a Vulcan Foundry set on the side of the smokebox and a Crewe or Armstrong Whitworth set on the frames.

BUILDER'S PLATES

The style and position of builder's plates differed: all engines built at Crewe, Derby and Horwich had oval plates fitted both sides to the front of the frames. Vulcan Foundry Nos 5020 to 5069 and Nos 5075 to 5106 had oval-pattern plates on both sides of the smokebox directly above the top of the steam pipe and above the ejector pipe; from No 5107 onwards the plates were attached to the front of the frames. The first six Armstrong Whitworth locomotives (Nos 5125 to 5130) had rectangular pattern plates on the smokebox in the

Above:
No 44878, fitted with a No 6 snowplough, at Gleneagles with an up passenger train, February 1964. (CR/KMF)

Left:
The Armstrong Whitworth (AW) Works plate as fitted to Nos 5125 to 5224 and Nos 5225 to 5451. It is believed that the plates were originally painted red, with polished brass lettering. The first AW locomotives (Nos 5125 to 5130) had the Works plates fitted to the sides of the smokebox but all subsequent AW locomotives had the plates in the more usual position on the front frames ahead of the smokebox. On the first engines the Works plates were later moved to the more usual position. (AC)

Above and Above Right:
Vulcan Foundry Works plate as fitted to Nos 5020 to 5069 and Nos 5075 to 5124. Up to No 5106 the plates were fixed to the side of the smokebox when built, but were soon moved to the more usual position on the frames.

Horwich LMS Works plate on No 44767 the Stephenson valve gear engine. The Works plates used by Crewe and Derby were similar. Those on engines built after nationalisation were similar. (both AC)

Above Right:
A view of the guard plate which stopped the screw-link coupling smashing into the AWS contact shoe bolted to the front of the bogie (the shoe is missing in this photograph). (AC)

same position as the Vulcan Foundry locomotives; on the remainder (Nos 5131 to 5451) the plates were attached to the front of the frames.

BUFFERBEAMS

The Crewe-built Short Firebox locomotives had flush-head rivets on the front bufferbeam whereas the corresponding Vulcan Foundry and Armstrong Whitworth-built versions had two large bolts at each end, as did all of the Long Firebox engines up to No 4805. Thereafter the bufferbeams had a large number of snaphead rivets, and many of the earlier locomotives received this pattern when overhauled in later years.

BOGIES

The 6ft 6in wheelbase bogie had 3ft 3½in diameter 10-spoked wheels and was derived from GWR practice, which itself was based on the bogie of the 1903 French-built de Glehn compound locomotive purchased by the GWR in 1904. These became known as 'French bogies'. The weight of the engine was transferred to the bogie through large circular friction pads. Side control was by helical springs mounted on either side of the centre casting.

The first 50 Vulcan Foundry locomotives (Nos 5020 to 5069) and the first four from Crewe (Nos 5000 to 5003) had large holes

Left:
The prototype Short Firebox engine No 5020 had a 27ft 2in wheelbase, 11ft 3in connecting rods, plain coupling rods, a cranked/flat combination lever, plain bearings on the eccentric return crank pin, an early-type crosshead with two-bolt arm fixing and a short union link with plain ends. It also had a solid cast valve spindle crosshead guides, a crosshead vacuum pump, plain balance weights and single brake shoes. The cylinder wrappers were plain. (AC)

Left:
No 5421, a Long Firebox engine of 1936, had a 27ft 2in wheelbase with 11ft 3in connecting rods, a straight fluted combination lever, a three-bolt drop arm crosshead, a crosshead vacuum pump and a short union link with plain ends. It also had plain coupling rods, riveted balance weights, plain bearings on the eccentric return crank pin, single brake shoes and solid cast valve spindle crosshead guides. There was a small circular plate in the cylinder clothing and rectangular cover plates on the shoulders. (AC)

through the bogie axles; the remaining engines had small centre turning. The axles with the large holes subsequently appeared on other engines, sometimes on one axle only.

WHEELS AND AXLES

The standard Stanier pattern 6ft 0in diameter 19-spoke wheels had triangular section rims and 3in tyres secured by Gibson rings. To save weight the coupled axles were 3in hollow bored throughout the length. The built-up balance weights were made from steel plates retaining a lead/antimony alloy with equivalent weights on the crankpins.

The first 70 locomotives (Nos 5000 to 5069) had stiffening webs fitted at the rear of the four spokes adjacent to the crankpin. These wheelsets did not always stay with the engines to which they were originally fitted and subsequently could be seen on other engines. Early engines could be fitted with wheels without the stiffening webs.

The Short Firebox locomotives originally had plain balance weights built up from steel plates which covered eight spokes on the middle (driving) axle and five spokes on the leading and trailing axles. All Long Firebox engine batches had riveted balance weights and did not have lightening holes bored through the axles. With the swapping of both wheelsets and axles, p.28 ▶

Right:
Built in 1947 No 4768 was one of the last 27ft 2in wheelbase engines. The main differences from No 5241 (opposite) were the shorter 10ft 10in connecting rods, the long union link with forked ends, and fluted coupling rods. It also had twin-articulated brake shoes, a fabricated crosshead, a large circular plate in the cylinder clothing and riveted balance weights. The eccentric return crank pin roller bearings had circular brass covers. (AC)

Right:
A later 27ft 6in wheelbase engine. The only difference from No 4758 (below) was the plain bearings throughout. (AC)

Right below:
No 4758 was fitted throughout with roller bearings and was the first of the 27ft 6in wheelbase engines. It had 10ft 10in connecting rods, fabricated valve spindle crosshead guides, a straight fluted combination lever, a three-bolt drop arm crosshead and long union link with forked ends. The cylinder clothing had a large circular access plate and rectangular cover plates on the shoulders. Also fitted were twin-articulated brake shoes, riveted balance weights, and circular brass covers over the eccentric return crank pin roller bearings. (AC)

Left:
The valve motion of No 45025 as built, showing the original type of combination lever with a forked lower end and cranked top. (AC)

Left centre:
The crosshead of an engine fitted with the later type of combination lever which is straight, fluted and without forked ends. Note also the single brake shoes and steam sanding pipes. (AC)

Below:
A diagram of Walschaerts valve gear showing all the component parts. The main component that differed between batches on the Class 5 was the combination lever. (AC)

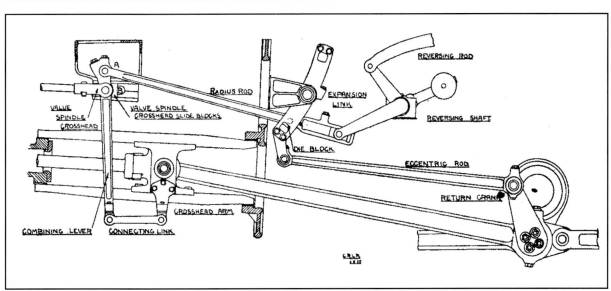

locomotives could be seen with some axles bored out and some not, and with both riveted and plain balance weights.

SANDING

Six sandboxes provided front sanding to the leading and driving coupled wheels and back sanding to the trailing pair. The four forward sandboxes were mounted within the frames and had filler necks and caps brought up through the running plate. On the Short Firebox engines the sand was applied to the rails by gravity, (known as trickle or gravity sanding) but this gave problems and was soon modified with a hot-water de-sanding device. This was mounted behind the coupled wheels, in each direction of travel to wash

sand off the rail head to prevent interference with track circuits. Gravity sanding was replaced by steam sanding from 1938 onwards and at the same time the hot-water de-sanding gear was removed.

All Long Firebox locomotives were built with steam sanding gear instead of the dry trickle or gravity sanding fitted on the Short Firebox engines.

CYLINDERS

The early Short Firebox locomotives had completely plain cylinder wrappers which allowed no access to the steam chest drain. A small circular cover plate with four fixing bolts, to provide access to the steam chest drain pipe (making it easier than removing the whole

Above:
View of the cylinder drain cocks fitted to No 45305. This also shows the lower end of the later type combination lever. (AC)

Left:
The arrangement of the vacuum pump driven by the crosshead. Note the bracket attached to the crosshead which drives the pump. When the pumps were removed the holes for the bracket in the crosshead remained. (AC)

cylinder wrapper), was introduced on locomotives built from June 1935 onwards, and in the period late 1930s to early 1940s a slightly larger cover was fitted. Two rectangular covers at the top of the wrapper were fitted to the Long Firebox locomotives and eventually all locomotives carried the later pattern covers.

The cylinder draincocks had vertical-type poppet valves and simple operating linkage. Three drain pipes were fitted to the front, middle and rear of each cylinder.

VALVE GEAR

The Walschaerts valve gear broadly followed existing LMS practice; a two-piece expansion link bolted together, with two bronze dieblocks, and four-stud fixing of the return cranks.

ECCENTRIC RODS/RETURN CRANKS

Engine Nos 5000 to 5451 had plain bearings to the eccentric-return crank pin but these were changed beginning with No 5452 to SKF roller bearings, which were fitted with distinctive circular brass covers.

COMBINATION LEVERS, CROSSHEAD AND UNION LINKS

The first two Short Firebox batches (Nos 5000 to 5069) had the Horwich type of combination lever. This was of plain rectangular section, offset below the spindle guide and forked at the lower end. The crosshead was of the early type with a two-bolt arm fixing and a short plain ended union link.

Right:
The front of No 5240. Note the following features: plain bufferbeam, smokebox door lug and steam heat pipe. The bottom of the smokebox door ring is riveted. (AC)

Far right:
No 44734 at Newton Heath, Manchester, in 1962. Note the door lug on the smokebox door, snaphead rivets on the bufferbeam, AWS protection plate and the steam heat pipes below the bufferbeam.(AC)

The later Short Firebox engines (Nos 5070 to 5224) had a straight, fluted combination lever with slight offset, still forked at the bottom pin, allowing use of the same union link and crosshead arm secured to the crosshead by two bolts as Nos 5000 to 5069.

All of the Long Firebox engines were fitted with a new pattern of straight-fluted combination lever which had forked-union links and was accompanied by a Derby-style three-bolt drop-arm crosshead.

The union links were changed to a longer pattern type with forked ends when shorter connecting rods were introduced from No 5472 onwards.

CROSSHEAD DRIVEN VACUUM PUMPS

Nos 5000 to 5451 were originally fitted with vacuum pumps driven off the left-hand crosshead. These were intended to maintain the vacuum in the train pipe when running but were unreliable and were removed over the period 1938 to 1941.

VALVE SPINDLE GUIDES

From No 4826 onwards the valve-spindle crosshead guides were changed from solid non-ferrous castings to an open steel fabricated type with flat guides spaced by bobbins.

COUPLING AND CONNECTING RODS

The coupling and connecting rods were made from manganese-molybdenum steel; the connecting rods were fluted and the fish-bellied profile coupling rods were plain rectangular in section on Nos 5000 to 5471. These were changed to fluted-section rods, slightly fish-bellied, on all subsequent locomotives.

From No 5472 onwards, the connecting rods were shortened by 5in to 10ft 10in centres with a consequent 5in increase in the length of the piston rods and union links. This was required, when changing the piston rings, to enable the piston head to be drawn clear of the cylinder without 'breaking' the piston rod joint to the crosshead. This resulted in two readily visible changes: the union link was lengthened and the slidebars projected further behind the motion plate.

On those engines with the lengthened frame the rear coupling rods were 3in longer than on the shorter wheelbase locomotives.

BRAKE BLOCKS

Nos 5000 to 5451 had 15in single cast-iron brake blocks which followed GWR practice, and were set at an incline of 1 in 20 to match the tyre tread taper. This required an p.34▶

Right:
The 6ft 6in wheelbase bogie of a Class 5 had 3ft 3in diameter wheels. The design was based on GWR practice which originated from a French-built 1903 De Glehn compound locomotive purchased by the GWR in 1904. (AC)

Left:
The frames and slide bar support brackets of the Class 5. Note the bogie wheel splasher which is not normally visible when all valve motion parts are in place. (AC)

Left:
The left-hand side step to the cab. Mounted behind is the injector. (AC)

Far left:
No 45305 showing the air tank for the AWS equipment mounted in front of the cab. Note the large holes bored through the driving wheel axle to reduce weight. Also fitted are single brake shoes and the modified spring hangers which were used after 1945. (AC)

Far left centre:
Roller bearings with large brass covers were fitted to the eccentric return cranks from No 5452 onwards. These replaced the plain bearings on earlier engines. (AC)

angular setting of the brake cross beam and hanger bracket ends.

The 20 locomotives built with single brake shoes were, in 1938, fitted with twin-brake shoes articulated on the hangers. These were fitted on all engines from No 5452 onwards.

BRAKE VALVES

The Short Firebox locomotives were fitted with the standard Gresham & Craven 'Dreadnought' combination driver's brake valve and ejector steam valve, instead of the normal LMS Midland-type fittings. These were replaced after the war by standard LMS brake valves with separate ejector steam control.

MECHANICAL LUBRICATORS

One of the few items that did not change over the life of the Class 5s was the use of two Silvertown-type mechanical lubricators mounted on the right-hand running plate (looking forward). Drive was taken from small crank arms on the inner trunnions on the rear of the expansion link by shaft and rocker to the lubricators. One lubricator with 12 feeds was for the cylinders (valve spindle and piston packing, cylinder barrel top and bottom, and front and back ends of the steamchest), the other of eight feeds was for the coupled axleboxes, each having an independent oil feed to the top of the axle box.

ATOMISERS

Each of the feeds for the cylinder lubrication was fitted with a standard LMS-design atomiser which was supplied with superheated steam through an elaborate system of check valves and piping. The superheated-steam pipe emerged on the left side of the smokebox above the handrail. The stop valve was fitted with a bullet-shaped cover.

A shorter pattern cover appeared on the Armstrong Whitworth Long Firebox boiler batch (Nos 5225 to 5451), and then from No 5452 onwards (including forward top-feed boilers), a 'streamlined' cover mounted further forward and below the handrail was fitted.

SPEED INDICATORS

The LMS experimented with speedometers in the late 1930s and a small number of Class 5s were fitted with British Thompson Houston (BTH) speed indicators, powered by an alternator mounted on a bracket suspended from the platform on the left-hand side immediately in front of the cab. The equipment proved unreliable and because spares in wartime were in short supply these were removed in the early 1940s.

In the late 1950s almost 100 of the class were planned to be fitted with the BR standard Smith-Stone equipment with the generator carried on a return crank on the left trailing crankpin, but the work was not fully completed because steam was beginning to be phased out.

SNOWPLOUGHS

Many of the Scottish-based locomotives were fitted in the winter with small front bufferbeam-mounted snowploughs for use on Highland lines. This equipment enabled Class 5s to pass through small snowdrifts, either whilst hauling normal trains or as a patrolling light engine. It also prevented the build-up of snow drifts which would otherwise cause a complete blockage if traffic ceased. Ploughs were also fitted to engines working in the more exposed parts of England such as the Settle to Carlisle line.

The original LMS snowploughs were based on a Caledonian Railway design and the No 5 nose plough was the one usually fitted to Class 5s. It was bolted to the front bufferbeam by means of two heavy steel angle uprights (that required three fixing bolts) approximately 12in inboard from the buffers. The bolt holes are visible on many photographs where the plough has been removed. A major problem with the No 5 plough was that it projected a long way in front of the engine which made it difficult to attach a pilot engine.

The No 5 plough was replaced in 1950 by the BR No 6 which was fixed at the bottom edge of the bufferbeam below the buffers. The advantage of the new No 6 plough was that it did not project beyond the buffers when they were compressed and therefore could be left in position throughout the winter. The ploughs could remain fitted so that two engines could be coupled smokebox to smokebox with the buffers fully compressed and without the ploughs coming into contact. For both types the front steam heating pipes had to be removed. The majority of engines with snowploughs were based at Inverness and Carlisle Kingmoor, but ploughs were also fitted to locomotives allocated to sheds such as North-ampton, Springs Branch, Preston and Patricroft.

Left:
No 45120 at Crewe South, November 1965, fitted with the BR No 6 snowplough. The engine has a domeless boiler, welded tender and carries overhead warning flashes. Note the lowered top lamp bracket. (AC)

CHAPTER THREE

CAB AND RUNNING PLATE

There were several subtle changes in the design
of the cab and the running plate; over time more noticeable
modifications were also applied to many of the class.

The cab was one of the few main components of each locomotive that did not change. Variants, over time, resulted from operational requirements and safety improvements.

CAB

The cabs were of Horwich style similar to the Stanier 2-6-0 mixed traffic engine, with two sliding windows, on each side, fitted in wooden frames of half-round section beading and radiused bottom corners. Also fitted were small hinged windows acting as draught preventers. Across the front of the cab above the firebox a series of 1in diameter holes was drilled to allow fresh air to pass along the inside of the roof, extra ventilation being provided by a sliding hatch in the roof. The vertical handrail at the rear of the cab side was fixed at the top to the beading which ran from the bottom edge of the cab roof down the rear of the sidesheet. At the bottom the handrail was bent at 90° and attached to the turn-in of the sidesheet.

When built, Nos 5020 to 5069 had no rain gutters above the side windows but these were added within the first two to three years in service.

From No 5452 onwards, the front windows were fixed and the wooden frame was omitted, flat beading with squared bottom corners being

used. A final change introduced from No 4826 was the fixing of the vertical handrail at the rear of the cab side to stanchions ('handrail knobs' in modeller's parlance) at both top and bottom.

FRONT PLATFORM STEP

All, apart from the first 25 Vulcan Foundry-built locomotives (Nos 5020 to 5044), were completed with a raised step between the frames below the smokebox front, which allowed easy access to the smokebox and top lamp bracket for footplate and shed staff. Steps were fitted to all Vulcan Foundry-built engines within the following two or three years.

CARRIAGE WARMING PIPES

All the first batch locomotives except those built by outside contractors (Nos 5020 to 5069 and Nos 5075 to 5224) were fitted with steam-heating pipes on the front bufferbeam, although in some cases these appeared and disappeared later, probably as a result of frame changes. A few of those with pipes had them removed (the holes for the bracket bolts are visible at the bottom of the bufferbeam), as when fitted with a snowplough. The flexible hoses were normally removed during the summer months when heating was not required.

Above:
No 45429 climbs to Beattock summit hauling a mixture of wagons on a through freight train, August 1962. (CR/TO)

Left:
No 5000 in preservation finished in LMS original livery. The sliding cab windows can be clearly seen and also the original method of attaching the vertical cab handrail. (AC)

Right:
The footplate and
cab front showing
the small AWS
cylinder and the
vacuum ejector
along the side
of the firebox. The
pipework clipped to
the edge of the
footplate is for the
AWS equipment.
(AC)

AWS EQUIPMENT

From 1957, BR standard Automatic Warning System (AWS) equipment was fitted to most of the class. The main visible features were a cylindrical vacuum reservoir on the right-hand side footplate immediately in front of the cab with a smaller timing reservoir on the left-hand side. The receiver was mounted on the front stretcher bar of the bogie with a guard plate under the front buffer beam to prevent the screw coupling damaging the receiver. A cable conduit was clipped to the outside edge of the left-hand side of the valance from the receiver to the cab, which also housed the battery box below the driver's seat.

TABLET EXCHANGE APPARATUS

One of the earliest modifications made to the class was the provision of tablet exchange apparatus on Scottish-based locomotives used on the single lines in the north. This was attached to the rear left-hand cabside at approximately running plate height.

The locomotives allocated to the Somerset & Dorset Joint Railway (S&DJR) line had Whittaker tablet apparatus fitted to the tender front at the left-hand side.

NAMES

Only four Class 5s were named while in revenue service, all in Scotland during the late 1930s

		Date
No 5154	*Lanarkshire Yeomanry*	8 April 1937
No 5156	*Ayrshire Yeomanry*	19 September 1936
No 5157	*The Glasgow Highlander*	6 March 1936
No 5158	*Glasgow Yeomanry*	22 May 1936

The nameplates were attached to backplates above the leading driving wheel and all had crests; that of No 5157 was mounted above the name, the other three below.

Far left:
No 45476 in 1960, showing the sliding cab windows but now with the cab handrails held by stanchions at the top and bottom. Note also the rubber extension to the bottom of the cab door. This was a standard fitment but appears to have disappeared quickly from most engines. (AC)

Far left centre:
The cab of No 4929 showing the two fall plates and the injectors behind both cab steps. (AC)

Left:
No 45327 at Crewe Works. It has sliding cab windows and the first style of vertical cab handrail fixing. The two fall plates are seen in a vertical position revealing the holes in the framework to reduce the weight of the engine. (AC)

Below:
The running plate and the sandbox filler caps and pipes. The pipe, along the footplate, passes under the boiler clothing to the topfeed. (AC)

Left:
No 44964 at the
Rugby shed, March
1953, in BR livery
with the early style
totem on the tender.
The engine is fitted
with a Long Firebox
boiler with the
topfeed on the
second ring of the
boiler. (CR/JMc)

Left:
The air tank for the
Automatic Warning
System (AWS)
equipment mounted
on the running plate
ahead of the cab. The
lid to the sandbox is
visible between the
wheels. (AC)

Right:
No 44711 at
Wakefield,
1 November 1965.
Note the fixed cab
windows and
stanchions to the cab
handrails. The
locomotive is a long-
wheelbase type and
has fluted coupling
rods, also AWS. It is
coupled to a part-
welded tender with
plain axleboxes and
external sieve boxes.
The engine is
finished in plain
black. (AC)

Right:
No 44765 is seen
when running with a
single chimney (when
various chimney
types were being
tested at Rugby in
1950). Also fitted is
electric lighting; the
steam generator is
behind the steam
pipes. The boiler has
the topfeed on the
first ring. When the
tests were completed
this engine reverted
to the original double
chimney until
withdrawal from
service. A part-
welded tender is
fitted. (AC)

Right:
No 5439 in 1936-
style LMS livery.
Visible are
the two lubricators
on the footplate.
A Long Firebox
boiler with topfeed
on the second ring
of the boiler is
fitted. (AC)

Left:
A scene taken in 1935 at Derby shed showing clearly how the sliding cab window is recessed into the cabside. (AC)

Left:
No 44694 at Leeds, 1962. Note the stanchions to the cab handrail and the flat beading fixed around the front window. The rubber extension fitted to the lower edge of the cab door is, as usual, missing. (AC)

CHAPTER FOUR

NON-STANDARD LOCOMOTIVES

Over 800 locomotives had the same Walschaerts valve gear
configuration; in late LMS days a small number of the
class were built with different valve gear which resulted
in a significant change in appearance.

In the last years of its existence the LMS
continued to search for increased availability
and reduced maintenance costs and the final
100 engines were subject to a wide range of
experiments, some of which have already been
described above. Twenty-three were built with
alternative types of valve gear in an attempt
to increase the mileage between valve
examinations. Except for the first of these, this
resulted in locomotives of radically different
appearance from the rest of the class, although
all had standard forward top feed Long Firebox
boilers, which they retained throughout, and
were paired with standard part-welded
tenders.

STEPHENSON VALVE GEAR

In late 1947 one of the class, No 4767, was built
with outside Stephenson-link valve gear driven
from double-return cranks with square fixings
with through bolts (not standard LMS practice).
The eccentric rods had plain bearings rather
than the roller type of contemporary Class 5s.

The locomotive included all the features
found on the standard longer wheelbase
Walschaerts valve gear Ivatt-designed engines but
also had electric lighting and a double chimney,
both of which were removed in the early 1950s.
Timken roller bearings were also fitted.

The drive to the mechanical lubricators on
the right-hand side was by a linkage from the
rear end of the back (outer) eccentric rod.

CAPROTTIS

In 1948 a total of 20 engines were built with
Caprotti poppet valve gear. All had the longer
wheelbase whilst the platforms and cab were
redesigned.

The side platforms, which were of lightweight
folded construction with no separate valance
angles, were lowered so that they were level with
the top of the valve box. Separate splashers were
fitted over the driving wheels. There was a short
front platform attached to the front buffer-beam
to allow access to the smokebox whilst the base of
the cab was level with the running plate; all of the
footsteps were of open construction.

The camboxes of the Caprotti gear were
mounted at the top of the cylinders, between the
poppet-valve spindles, but the drive shaft to the
camboxes from the leading coupled axle was
mounted between the frames. Bulbous-shaped
outside steam pipes fed to the front of the
cylinders; on Nos 4738 to 4747 these were
straight, whereas on the Timken roller bearing
fitted Nos 4748 to 4757 (with the drive-gear on
the top of the cannon boxes), the pipes were
cranked just above the cylinders.

Above:
No 44752 on a train of soda ash hoppers at Chinley Junction East, August 1963. Clearly visible are the 'cranked'-style of steam pipes fitted to the first ten Caprotti engines. (CR/PH)

Left:
The Stephenson valve gear on No 44767. Note also the drive to the two lubricators. (GM)

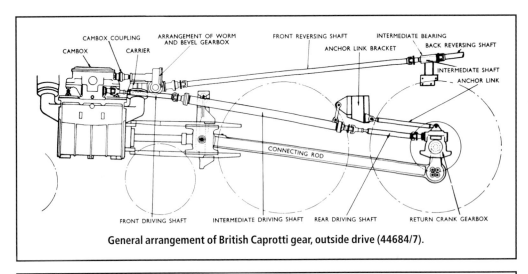

CAMBOX COUPLING   ARRANGEMENT OF WORM   FRONT REVERSING SHAFT   INTERMEDIATE BEARING
CAMBOX   CARRIER   AND BEVEL GEARBOX   ANCHOR LINK BRACKET   BACK REVERSING SHAFT
INTERMEDIATE SHAFT
ANCHOR LINK
CONNECTING ROD
FRONT DRIVING SHAFT   INTERMEDIATE DRIVING SHAFT   REAR DRIVING SHAFT   RETURN CRANK GEARBOX

General arrangement of British Caprotti gear, outside drive (44684/7).

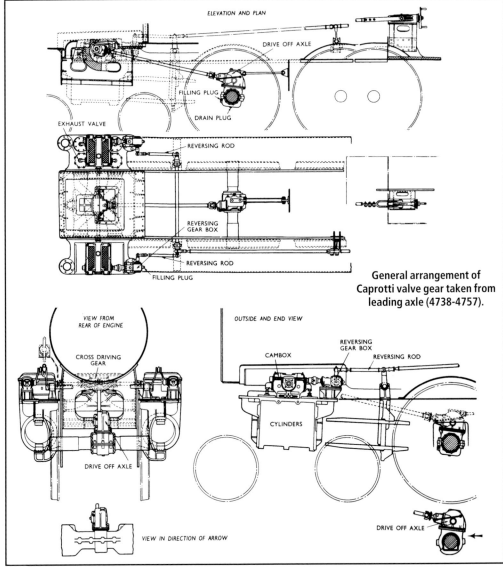

ELEVATION AND PLAN

DRIVE OFF AXLE

FILLING PLUG

DRAIN PLUG

EXHAUST VALVE

REVERSING ROD

REVERSING
GEAR BOX

REVERSING ROD

FILLING PLUG

General arrangement of Caprotti valve gear taken from leading axle (4738-4757).

VIEW FROM
REAR OF ENGINE

CROSS DRIVING
GEAR

OUTSIDE AND END VIEW

REVERSING
GEAR BOX
CAMBOX   REVERSING ROD

CYLINDERS

DRIVE OFF AXLE

VIEW IN DIRECTION OF ARROW

DRIVE OFF AXLE

This page:
The valve gear of
No 44767. Clearly
visible are the
twin-brake shoes.
The upper
photograph
illustrates how the
lubricators were
driven from the
crank axle. (both AC)

The boiler had to be pitched 2in higher than on the piston valve Class 5s to provide clearance for the cross-drive gearbox mounted beneath the smokebox. The height to the chimney top now increased to 12ft 10in. The poppet valves did not require an atomised oil supply and so there was no atomiser steam cock on the side of the smokebox. However the valves did require a steam supply to lift them on to their seatings when the regulator was open, and this was provided by an external pipe from the left-hand side of the dome.

There was a tubular reversing reach rod from the cab to the reversing gearbox above the rear of the left-hand cylinder; the gearbox on the other side was operated by a cross drive from below the front of the boiler. There were two mechanical lubricators on the right-hand running plate driven from a return crank on the driving crankpin.

Engine Nos 4748 to 44754 were built with short sandbox filler necks, which made filling extremely difficult because the filler caps were below the reversing reach rod. Beginning with No 44755, the necks on the left-hand side only were raised to bring the filler caps above the reach rod, and this was continued on Nos 44738 to 44747. The short sandbox filler necks on Nos M4748 to 44754 were replaced very quickly with the longer type.

Engine Nos 44755 to 44757 were fitted with double chimneys and, until the mid-1950s, electric-lighting equipment powered by a Stone turbo-generator mounted on a bracket low down on the right-hand side of the smokebox.

p.50 ▶

Above:
Caprotti engine No 44738 at Llandudno Junction, August 1959. It is finished in standard BR livery with a late-style totem on the tender. Note the 'straight'-style steam pipes. (CR/GHH)

Right:
No 44755 at Holbeck shed, Leeds, 21 September 1960, and fitted with a double chimney. The engine has the 'cranked'-style of steam pipes. (GM)

Above:
No 44748 on an express passenger train, picking up water at Castlethorpe Troughs, August 1958. The engine is fitted with a single chimney and 'cranked'-style steam pipes. (CR/TO)

Left:
One of the final two Class 5s built, Caprotti engine No 44686 in store at Llandudno junction in the 1960s (sacking over the chimney indicates storage). It has 'straight'-style steam pipes and a high-level running plate. (CR)

Right:
No 44767 at Carlisle Kingmoor, fitted with a single chimney. The engine has a Long Firebox boiler with topfeed on the first ring. It is coupled to a part-welded tender with roller-bearing axleboxes and external sieve boxes. AWS equipment is fitted. (AC)

Right:
No M4752 soon after completion in transitional livery of plain black common at that time. British Railways is painted on the tender but with M4752 on the cabside. It has the 'cranked'-style of steampipes. Note the pipe from the dome which supplied steam to enable the valves to be 'lifted' when running with steam shut off.
It has a part-welded tender with roller bearing axleboxes and external sieve boxes. (AC)

⏐ FINAL TWO CAPROTTIS ⏐

In 1951 the final two Caprotti Class 5s (Nos 44686 and 44687) were completed, the last of the LMS-type Class 5s to be built.

These had a modified type of Caprotti gear in which the drive to the camboxes was simplified with a separate outside drive to each cambox, which eliminated the cross-shaft drive under the smoke-box of the earlier engines. The camshafts were driven by outside shafts from return cranks on the driving crankpins. To allow

for this the drive to the mechanical lubricators had to be moved back to the right-hand trailing crankpin.

The revised layout of the Caprotti gear around the cylinders necessitated the side platforms to be set high over the camboxes. The platforms (now without splashers) were carried on brackets attached to the boiler. Both engines were fitted with a double chimney, and continued with the bulbous-shaped straight outside steam pipes used on Nos 4738 to 4747.

Left:
The sole Stephenson valve gear Class 5, No 44767 on a through freight train at Rodley near Leeds, 14 June 1967. The top lamp holder or iron on the smokebox has been moved to the lower position and AWS is fitted. It still retains a part-welded tender with roller-bearing axleboxes and external sieve boxes. (GM)

Left:
One of the last two Caprottis. Note the drive to the lubricators from the rear axle by a series of cranks and rods. The later BR Standard Class 5 locomotives fitted with Caprotti valve gear were virtually identical to these last two engines. (IA)

Right:
No 44738 at Crewe,
February 1950. The
reach rod which
controlled events on
the Caprotti valves
was different on this
engine compared
with all the other
Caprottis: it was
thicker and rose to the
cab front at a steeper
angle. A part-welded
tender is fitted. (AC)

Below:
Caprotti engine
No 44753 on a freight
train near Orton
Bridge, February
1963. (CR/MC)

Left:
The smokebox of No 44767 when in preservation. Clearly visible is the external feedpipe to the steam lance cock on the side of the smokebox. Also visible is the steam generator and electric lighting which was re-installed after preservation. (AC)

This page:
No 44756 at Holbeck
shed, Leeds, 12 April
1962. Visible is the
cam-box cover for
the Caprotti valves,
also the external
feedpipe to the
steam lance cock
on the side of the
smokebox. (GM)

Left:
No 44757 with the
'cranked'-style of
steam pipes and a
double chimney at
Holbeck shed, Leeds,
14 September 1963.
(GM)

Left:
The double cranks
are arranged to
drive the Stephenson
valve gear. (AC)

CHAPTER FIVE

TENDERS

The class ran with all three types of the standard
Stanier 4,000-gallon tender as it evolved over the years;
a small number of engines had experimental or unusual tenders.

The combination of Class 5 and standard Stanier 4,000-gallon tender was almost universal throughout the life of the class. However, there was a considerable amount of swapping during works visits because tenders took less time to repair than the locomotives and so a repaired engine would usually be fitted with the next available spare tender, not necessarily the one with which it entered the works.

RIVETED TENDERS

Engine Nos 5000 to 5124 were built with riveted tank tenders; the only visual difference was in the axlebox covers on Nos 5020 to 5069 which were flat-faced; the remainder had a crucifix pattern and these used on all other non-roller bearing tenders, irrespective of tank type.

WELDED TENDERS

All of the other pre-war engines (Nos 5125 to 5471) and the first wartime batch (Nos 5472 to 5499 and Nos 4800 to 4806) had a revised design with all-welded tanks which reduced the overall weight by over 1 ton.

PART-WELDED TENDERS

Problems developed with the seams of the all-welded tenders; from No 4826 onwards the design of the tanks was again changed, now being part-welded and part riveted to overcome the leakage problem. These tenders had a revised pattern of vents: the two tall 'mushroom'-shaped pipes were replaced by two rectangular pipes welded to the bunker backplate. The type could also be distinguished from the fully-riveted tender by the absence of the horizontal lines of rivets immediately above the base and at tank top level.

From No 4997 onwards external sieve boxes to trap sediment were introduced; these were mounted on a plate in the 'D' shaped opening in the frames between the leading and middle axleboxes.

In 1947 following the experimental fitting of roller-bearing axleboxes to 20 new engines the corresponding batch of part-welded tenders was also fitted with Timken roller-bearing axleboxes. These had circular-shaped axlebox covers and shorter spring hangers, in BR days the covers were painted yellow with a horizontal red stripe to identify the different type of bearing fitted.

The shorter spring hangers were also fitted to the subsequent non-roller bearing tenders.

STANIER - CONVERTED PROTOTYPE TENDERS

Three prototype 'flat-sided' tenders (Nos 9000 to 9002) were built in 1933 for the first two p.64 ▶

Left:
No 44664 at Nottingham Midland with a part-welded tender fitted with standard plain bearing axleboxes (as fitted to riveted and welded versions). The part-welded tenders also had external sieve boxes allowing shed staff to clean the water tank filters without having to enter the tender. (CR/FH)

Below:
No 44720 in the 1960s fitted with a riveted tender and AWS. Note the large cabside numerals and the late BR totem. (AC)

Right:
No 5016 as built with a domeless boiler and 4,000-gallon riveted tender. This was the 'standard' tender for most of the Stanier classes, even the 'Duchess' and 'Princess' tenders were based on this design, only the coal capacity being different. (AC)

Right centre:
No 44971 in 1947 fitted with one of two 1946 coal-weighing tenders introduced after World War Two. These were designed to allow the accurate weighing of coal consumed under test conditions. Two were built in 1946 and a further two in 1950. Water capacity was reduced to 3,750 gallons. The livery is typical of the transitional period with BR-style numerals on the cab but 'LMS' on the tender. (AC)

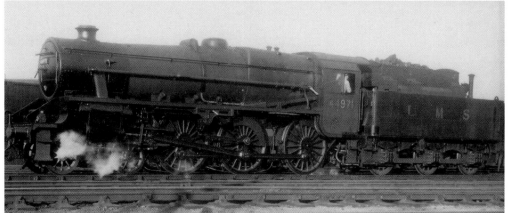

Right:
No 4774 at Sheffield, 9 July 1948, with its original part-welded tender. It is finished in 1946-style LMS livery. It has plain-bearing axleboxes and external sieve boxes. (AC)

Left:
No 44716 at Birmingham New Street coupled to a part-welded tender with plain-bearing axleboxes and external sieve boxes. The livery is BR with an early totem on the tender. The air vents on a part-welded tender were different to those on a riveted and welded tender, being a flat-shaped casing welded to the rear of the bunker. (AC)

Left:
No 45396 fitted with a riveted tender. (AC)

Left:
No 44684 fitted with a part-welded tender with roller-bearing axleboxes and external sieve boxes. Note the over-head warning flashes positioned adjacent to the rear steps. (AC)

Left:
No 44825 on an enthusiasts' special of brake vans at Gedling, Nottingham, coalfield in 1966. The welded tender is finished in BR black with a late-style totem. Overhead warning flashes are positioned on the rear of tender. (AC)

Far left top:
A welded tender showing the position of the toolboxes. The cover over the lamp bracket was to protect the lamp from damage when the tender is filled with coal. (AC)

Far left bottom:
No 44735 at Bolton le Sands, 29 March 1968, at the very end of steam services. A part-welded tender fitted with standard axleboxes and external sieve box is coupled to the engine. It is in very grimy condition with the BR totem barely visible. The hatch for the water filler has been left in the open position, a practice not unusual during the final years of steam. (AC)

Left:
No 44677 at Farrington, September 1963, fitted with a coal-weighing tender. (CR/MC)

Left:
The tender for
No 45110, showing
how one headlamp
could be stowed at
the top left of the
tender. The second
lamp is below.
Clearly visible are
the intermediate
buffers, and at the
left the tunnel for
stowage of the
fire-irons. (IA)

Far left:
One of the
experimental 4,000-
gallon tenders. If this
is compared to the
photograph opposite
it shows the different
intermediate buffers,
also a different
arrangement of the
tool box. (AC)

Right:
No 45493 at
Weymouth on the
Southern Region
being serviced after
hauling an LCGB
Special on 3 July
1966. In the 1960s it
was fashionable to
use locomotives
from other regions to
haul special trains.
This resulted in 'A4s'
and 'A2s' running on
the Southern and
rebuilt 'Merchant
Navy' engines
working on the
London Midland
Region. The rear of
the welded tender is
clearly shown here;
note the overhead
warning flashes
positioned adjacent
to the top steps to
warn staff of
overhead electric
cables close above.
(AC)

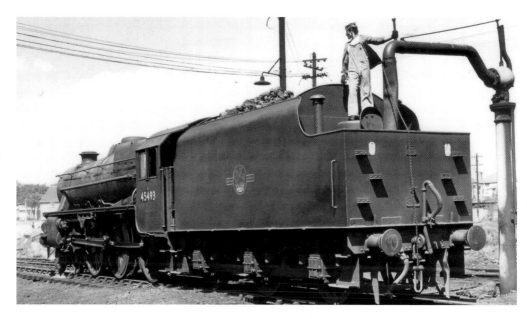

'Princess' class 4-6-2s (Nos 6200 to 6201) and for the US tour of *Royal Scot* (No 6100). These were rebuilt with curved upper sides in 1935 and attached to Crewe-built Class 5s, Nos 5073, 5074 and 5000. Although these looked similar to the standard 4,000-gallon riveted tender all were subtly different. All had most of the later standard features such as a 15ft equally divided wheelbase, but the rivet pattern and the curved cut-out at the top of the side panelling were different. Nos 9000 to 9002 were fitted with Timken roller bearings, distinguishable by their complex-pattern axlebox covers. The tenders were paired with the following locomotives:

No 9000 5073 (5/6/35-12/10/44),
5312 (28/10/44-30/6/45), 5144
(30/6/45-9/8/45), 5298 (21/3/46-
30/6/58), 5216 (23/1/59-27/2/61),
5249 (21/7/61-10/12/66).
No 9001 5074 (12/6/35-31/7/45),
5002 (31/7/45-19/1/46),
5146 (19/1/46-19/6/65).

Right:
No 45459 at
Polmadie, Glasgow,
16 May 1959, fitted
with a part-welded
tender painted with
a late-style BR
totem. Clearly visible
are the revised air
vents to the tender.
The locomotive has
large numerals
which were applied
to many locomotives
overhauled at
Scottish works. (AC)

No 9002   5000 (23/2/35–16/2/43),
          5147 (16/2/43–21/6/44),
          5198 (21/6/44–30/9/67).

COAL-WEIGHING TENDERS

Two coal weighing tenders, Nos 10590 and 10591, were built with engine Nos 4965 and 4966 at Horwich in 1946 at the request of the LMS Motive Power Department to enable the department to carry out simple coal consumption tests. There was a requirement to compare coal from different sources at a time when the cost was rapidly rising and quality was becoming more variable.

On these tenders the bunker was narrower than the water tank, straight sided and with covers at the side and back for the weighted steelyard. The water capacity was reduced from 4,000 to 3,750 gallons.

Two further coal weighing tenders, Nos 10836 and 10837, were built in 1950 with

Nos 44696 and 44697; these were similar to the first two built but the bunkers held slightly more coal, also the steelyard casing was smaller.

All four of these tenders had an external sieve box similar to, but smaller than, those fitted to later, part–welded tenders. In later years the steelyard and covers were removed, thus eliminating the ability to weigh coal. A fire iron tunnel was also added.

These tenders were attached to the following locomotives:

Tender No 10590

No 4965 (2/8/46 to 19/10/46), No 44986 (19/10/46 to 1/12/63), No 45081 (1/12/63 to 25/1/64), No 44986 (25/1/64 to 6/5/67).

Tender No 10591

No 4966 (10/8/46 to 26/11/46), No 4971 (26/11/46 to 9/5/47), No 4901 (9/5/47 to 23/5/47), No 5462 (23/5/47 to 25/5/47), No 4923 (25/5/47 to 28/5/47), No 4995 (28/5/47 to 20/8/47), No 4901 (20/8/47 to 26/8/47), No 44971 (26/8/47 to 12/2/58), No 45298 (30/6/58 to 16/9/67).

Left:
The standard axlebox cover fitted to welded and riveted tenders. For part-welded tenders with the standard axlebox the spring hangers are similar to those used on roller-bearing axlebox tenders. These hangers were shorter and had a different arrangement of bracket and fixing to the tender frames. (AC)

Tender No 10836

No 44696 (12/12/50 to 24/1/51), No 44697 (24/1/51 to 18/11/67).

Tender No 10837

No 44697 (27/12/50 to 11/6/54), No 44677 (11/6/54 to 4/11/62).

CORRIDOR TENDER

The former corridor tender, No 4999, was attached to engine No 45235 from 11/12/59 to 15/1/66. This experimental tender had been built in 1938 with a water capacity of 3,500 gallons. It was rebuilt in the 1950s with a part-welded 4,000-gallon body with flat-shaped air vents. The tender was distinguishable by the frames which had four small cut-outs on each side instead of two as on the standard tenders.

OIL BURNING

Five engines (Nos 4826, 4827, 4829, 4830 and 4844) were converted to oil firing in 1947, the tenders of which were fitted with oil tanks, but the equipment was removed the following year (1948) when the experiment was abandoned.

Below:
No 45198 with No 9002, one of the experimental tenders, on the West Coast main line at Blisworth near Northampton, 1957. (AC)

CHAPTER SIX

LIVERIES

Although named after its colour scheme,
the class carried a wide variety of liveries under both
LMS and BR ownership; only four were named and
another four were painted green for a few months.

Throughout service all Class 5s were painted black (with four exceptions) but insignia and lining changed over the years. This chapter is a short summary of this complex subject, because an individual locomotive could be finished in a 'hybrid' variant of the liveries described. Of the 842 locomotives built, 748 carried LMS and BR livery and 94 carried only BR livery.

LMS

When new, all the Short Firebox locomotives carried the LMS 1928-style fully-lined black livery with 12in cab numbers, 14in tender letters and 5P5F power designation in 3in letters. The characters were scroll and serif, gold shaded with bright vermilion to the right and crimson lake shading below. Scroll-pattern lettering was used for the front numberplate. The only variations were on the Vulcan Foundry-built engines (Nos 5020 to 5069 and Nos 5075 to 5124) which had lining around all four edges of the cab side sheet and below the cab windows; all others had conventional lining carried straight to the cab roof. The space between the tender LMS lettering was 60in except for Nos 5020 to 5069, Nos 5075 to 5111 and Nos 5125 to 5136, where this was 40in.

The first Long Firebox engines, the Armstrong Whitworth-built batch (Nos 5225 to 5451), were given the new-style 1936 LMS livery; the serif characters were changed throughout to sans serif and the cab numbers were reduced to 10in; the front numberplate lettering was now block style. A small number of the Short Firebox engines were repainted in this style, including most of those converted to Long Firebox boilers, but the LMS decided to revert back to the serif-type style in 1937.

Most repaints from that date had the new serif-pattern characters in yellow with plain vermilion shading and the final pre-World War Two batch (Nos 5452 to 5471) was finished in this livery. In Scotland some repaints used 10in gold characters, probably to use up old transfer stock.

The next change came in 1940 when the 5P5F power classification on the cab sidesheets was reduced to a simple numeral '5'. During World War Two all repaints were in plain unlined black, but it is likely that many engines were never fully repainted and kept the original lining. This style continued after the war with yellow sans serif or serif characters (plain or red-shaded), often with the cab numbers immediately below the side windows.

The final LMS livery of unlined black appeared in 1946; the characters were sans serif painted in pale straw colour with inset p.74▶

Above:
No 45430 ex-works
at Holyhead shed,
September 1953, in
clean BR lined livery
with an early-style
totem on the tender.
(CR/KC)

Left centre:
No 5001 as built in
1935 with domeless
boiler and riveted
tender. Note the scroll
and serif style of
lettering. (AC)

Left:
No 45461 on a
passenger train. The
locomotive has not
been cleaned
recently. It is fitted
with a Short Firebox
boiler (with only the
top-feed cover)
having originally
been built with a
Long Firebox boiler.
This was one of three
locomotives built as a
Long Firebox engine
to receive a Short
Firebox. (AC)

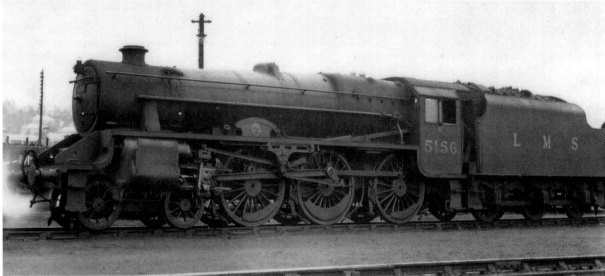

Above
No 5156 *Ayrshire Yeomanry* in September 1936 finished in sans-serif LMS livery. The locomotive is as built with a domeless boiler, and welded tender. (AC)

Right:
No 5154 in as-built condition with dome-less boiler and welded tender. The name *Lanarkshire Yeomanry* was applied in April 1937. (AC)

Far left:
No 5078 as delivered from Vulcan Foundry in March 1935, with a domeless boiler, crosshead vacuum pump and a riveted tender with LMS lettering closely spaced at 40in. (AC)

Left:
No 5484 photographed during the 1940s. Note the fluted coupling rods and Long Firebox with second ring topfeed (AC)

Left:
No 5112 at Stafford, 26 June 1948. Note the LMS scroll-style numerals on the plate fitted to the smokebox, also the letter 'M' on the cabside. (AC)

Below:
No 4870 photographed in the 1940s. (AC)

Right:
No 44997 at Perth, 1965, showing to perfection the BR lined livery with the later style totem and large cab numbers. It has a Long Firebox boiler with topfeed on second ring. The part-welded tender has standard axleboxes. Note the overhead warning flashes, and front lamp bracket still at the top of the smokebox door. The cylinder wrapping is unlined. (AC)

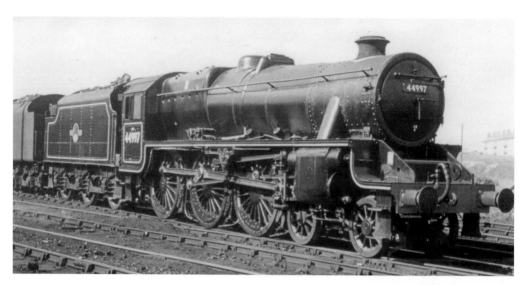

Above:
No 45010 at St Rollox, 1959, in late BR lined livery with a later totem on the tender. The engine is very much as built with a riveted tender and domeless boiler. (AC)

Right:
No 44979 at Perth, September 1964. AWS equipment is fitted as is tablet exchange apparatus. Note the late totem on the tender.(AC)

Above:
No 45011 at Perth, September 1964. This locomotive was built with a domeless boiler but is seen here with one of St Rollox Works 'specials': that of a topfeed cover from a domed boiler. No 45011 had an interesting history as it was converted from Short Firebox to Long Firebox then back to a Short Firebox. (AC)

Left:
No 5000 as preserved by the National Railway Museum and in original LMS livery. (AC)

Above:
No 44998 at Perth, 1948. It has one of the transitional liveries with full LNWR-style lining but with 'British Railways' on the tender rather than a BR totem. The engine has tablet exchange apparatus and fixed front cab windows. The power classification 5 is below the engine's number on the cab side. (AC)

Right:
No 45177 at Balornock, Glasgow, in 1958. This locomotive was originally built with a Short Firebox but was converted to a Long Firebox. Note the topfeed on the first ring of the boiler. The totem is of the early-BR type even though this style had been replaced in 1957. (AC)

maroon lining. Lettering on the tender was 14in and cab numbers were originally 12in painted in the high position below the cab windows; some later had 10in numerals. This livery first appeared on No 4997 and was applied up to No 4767; other than these new engines, only a few were repainted in the new livery.

BRITISH RAILWAYS

Following an inspection by BR officials of three Class 5s painted in Southern Railway (SR), GWR and London & North Eastern Railway (LNER) green liveries and one in London & North Western Railway (LNWR) lined black, the latter was selected as the new BR standard mixed-traffic locomotive livery in early 1948.

Thus the whole class eventually carried LNWR-style lined black mixed-traffic livery, but in the first two years after nationalisation several different styles of insignia were used. The cab numbers initially had an 'M' above or below the engine's number, at first with no insignia and then with 'BRITISH RAILWAYS' in full on the tender. The M prefix was soon

Left:
A Caprotti locomotive, No 44756, fitted with a double chimney. The smokebox number plate is the standard Gill Sans type, also note the SC plate indicating a self-cleaning smokebox. Also clearly visible are the 'cranked'-style steam pipes. (GM)

replaced by adding 40,000 to the number. New Class 5s built between July 1948 and July 1949 followed the same pattern; from No 44668 in December 1949 the final black lined livery with the first version of the British Railways emblem was applied.

There were several variations of BR cab side numbers at this time with large and small numbers applied at various heights on the cab side; some had the numeral 4 prefix spaced away from the other four numerals and sometimes it was in a much smaller size. All lettering and numbers were in Gill Sans typeface finished in cream, edged with a narrow black band. The final style of numerals adopted for the cab sides were 8in high, although many of those shopped in Scotland received larger 10in numerals. The tenders received both styles of BR emblem in turn.

The lining on the cab and tender sides was painted with the broad grey line on the outside, edged with the narrow cream band inside. The red line was further inside, spaced away from the one in cream. On the valances, p.79▶

LMS 1928 insignia
1234567890

5 Power classifications 1928

5 Power classifications 1936

L M S 1234567890
1936 insignia

LMS 1234567890
1946 insignia

Left:
No 45292 at Marylebone, April 1948. The locomotive and tender are finished in BR lined black livery. Note the lining on the edge of the cabside and continued up to the roof. This was soon changed to the usual lines panel below the windows. The tender underframe was also lined in grey and cream. (CR/DOW)

Below:
No 45158 *Glasgow Yeomanry,* one of only four Class 5 locomotives to be named. St Rollox shed, October 1963. (CR/AS)

Right:
No 45156 *Ayrshire Yeomanry*, named in September 1936. In the last years of service this engine had the nameplates removed. Later, shed staff painted the name onto the backing plate. It is finished in the final-style BR livery with a late totem on the tender. (AC)

The official BR specification for the lining style for Class 5 mixed traffic livery.

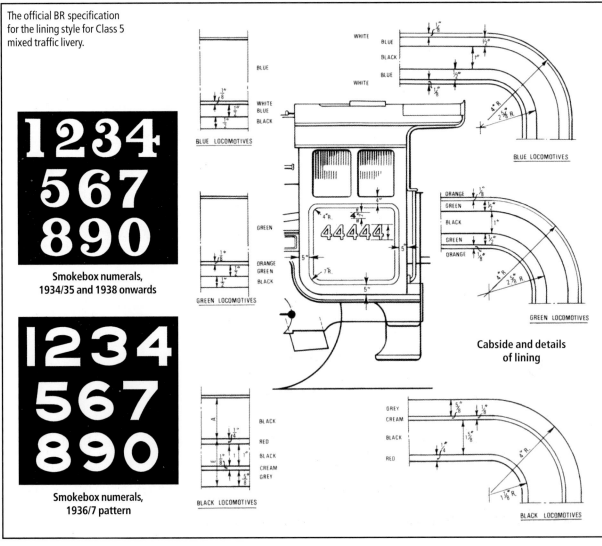

Smokebox numerals, 1934/35 and 1938 onwards

Smokebox numerals, 1936/7 pattern

BLUE LOCOMOTIVES

GREEN LOCOMOTIVES

BLACK LOCOMOTIVES

BLUE LOCOMOTIVES

GREEN LOCOMOTIVES

BLACK LOCOMOTIVES

Cabside and details of lining

Left:
No 44831 in unlined black livery introduced at the end of 1963. Black was painted over the original lining and some engines when cleaned for enthusiasts' specials had the paint rubbed off to reveal the lining. As usual for a locomotive surviving into the last days of steam the top lamp bracket on the smokebox door has been lowered. (AC)

Left:
No 45312 ex-works at Springburn shed, 22 March 1964, after overhaul at Cowlairs. Built as a Long Firebox locomotive with topfeed on the second ring, No 45312 has now been fitted with a Long Firebox boiler with topfeed on the first ring. Interestingly the locomotive has been fully lined. This was some months after the instruction was issued to repaint engines plain black only. Note the large cabside number with the locomotive power classification above the number. (GM)

the lining was the same, with the grey line at the bottom edge of the valance. Boiler clothing bands were edged with two red lines, as were bands on the cylinder covers.

The cast numberplate on the smokebox door also varied during the re-numbering from LMS to BR with a few engines having scroll-style numerals. These were generally changed to the standard sans serif pattern within a few years. The numbers were painted white on a black background; some Scottish Region engines had a blue background and a few that were based in England had a red background.

In the period late 1950s to the early 1960s the power classification on the cabside was changed to 5MT and 'electric overhead' warning plates were applied to those parts of the locomotive where footplate crews would be near to the overhead wires.

In the latter years many Class 5s lost the lining out on the cylinder cover bands, and from December 1963 locomotives receiving a full repaint were to be finished in plain black. However, locomotives outshopped from St. Rollox in Scotland were still being lined out in early 1964.

In addition to the shed plate fitted to the smokebox door, Scottish sheds (and some English) also had the home shed name painted in full on the bufferbeam. This practice appears to have been confined to the Cowlairs works.

CHAPTER SEVEN

IN SERVICE

The Class 5 exemplified the term 'mixed traffic',
working all over the country on virtually every type
of train; it replaced many pre-Grouping designs and
survived until the final days of BR steam.

The Class 5 was ubiquitous; it could be found nearly everywhere on a wide range of duties,

ALLOCATIONS AND WORKINGS

The early batches of Class 5s went to those districts which were in most urgent need of modern motive power to replace older mainly pre-Grouping locomotives. One of the most pressing requirements was in the north of Scotland and the first engines from Vulcan Foundry were delivered to Perth and Inverness. As more of the Short Firebox locomotives were delivered these went to the Western and Central Divisions, replacing large numbers of ex-LNWR locomotives, and to provide increased power capacity on the Midland Division.

By the end of 1937 over 450 engines were in service and were dispersed all over the LMS system. They were used on almost every type of working from local and unfitted freights to express passenger duties. The Class 5 fully justified the mixed traffic designation.

After the war as more locomotives came into service the Class 5 continued to take over duties from older types and was to remain the backbone of the LMR fleet up to the very end of BR steam services in 1968.

WITHDRAWALS

The first withdrawal was No 45401 in November 1961 following a collision. Regular withdrawals began in 1962 with the final 46 engines being taken out of service in August 1968.

Interestingly, no effort was made to take out of service early the older small-grate Short Firebox engines, over 30 of which were in service until 1968; the non-standard only survived until 1966.

PRESERVATION

Of the class, 18 have survived; for modellers interested in using these for examining details they should be treated with caution. Those rescued from the Barry scrapyard have had many missing parts replaced during preservation and a number of modifications have also been made, such as the fitting of rocker ashpans, to improve operational efficiency. Tenders have also been given greater water capacity and air pumps fitted to allow working with air-braked coaching stock, and TWPS installed for mainline operation:
Short Firebox : Nos 5000, 5025, 5110, 5163, and 5212. Long Firebox : Nos 4806, 4871, 4901, 4932, 5231, 5293, 5305, 5337, 5379, 5407, 5428, and 5491. Stephenson valve gear: No 4767
None of the Caprotti or long-wheelbase Walschaerts locomotives has survived.

This page: No 44737 at Liverpool Exchange with a Blackpool express, April 1954, with the safety valves lifting. The fireman would be reprimanded by a locomotive inspector for blowing off the safety valves in the station. All over the network Class 5s could be seen working express trains on a daily basis right up to the end of steam in 1968. (CR)

Right:
No 5126 at Hellifield in June 1937 running under express passenger headlamp code but as a special train (indicated by the number on the smokebox door). This is confirmed by the use of ex-Midland Railway stock at the front of the train. At this time 'normal' express trains were generally composed of more modern steel coaches. (AC)

Right:
No 44733 on an express freight train at Lune Gorge, 18 August 1962. (GM)

Left:
A classic view of No 5366 on an express freight. The Class 5 was as comfortable on fast freights as on passenger trains. Many of the initial allocations were to sheds to specifically run fast freights of this type. (AC)

Right:
No 44982 at Carlisle, June 1956, with the 5pm train to Preston. The carriages are the last set of Maryport & Carlisle narrow-bodied rolling stock in service. (CR/RO)

Below:
No 44775 on shed in April 1961 waiting for the next turn of duty, which for a Class 5 could be anything from the lowly ballast train up to an express passenger train. As late as Easter 1968, Class 5s were working the Preston to Liverpool sections of Glasgow to Liverpool expresses. The locomotive is in late BR condition with lowered top lamp bracket and a speedometer. Whilst authority had been given to fit a large number of Class 5s with speedometers, only a small proportion ever received the equipment. (AC)

Left:
No 44976 on the Highland line passing through Glen Douglas with a Queen Street to Fort William express passenger train, September 1959. The Class 5s when first introduced were allocated to the ex-Highland lines and revolutionised the operations, replacing pre-Grouping locomotives. The Class 5 soon became the standard engine on those lines. (CR/TJE)

Left:
Class 5s at Chester station in 1964. No 45045 is seen entering from the Manchester/Crewe direction with an express passenger train almost certainly for Holyhead or the North Wales coast to Llandudno. The locomotive has had the boiler changed since building. It originally had a domeless boiler but now has a separate dome and topfeed. Across the tracks, two Class 5s, one of which is now preserved (No 45305), are coupled together, probably to move to Chester depot (6A) for servicing and preparation for the next duties. Class 5s were popular with the crews on the North Wales coast on the tightly timed Llandudno to Manchester club train (and return) and were preferred to 'Britannia' Pacifics allocated to Bangor at that time. Chester on a summer Saturday would see a non-stop stream of Class 5s on holiday excursion trains as well as regular workings. Chester, Llandudno junction and Bangor all had sizable allocations of these capable engines. (AC)

Right:
An atmospheric
shot of a Class 5,
No 45447, on shed
at Rose Grove,
10 June 1968. (GM)

Above:
No 44767, the Stephenson valve gear locomotive, and No 44916 in the roundhouse of Holbeck shed, Leeds, 15 June 1967. Both engines are fitted with AWS and have lowered top lamp brackets. (GM)

Left:
No 44767, the only Class 5 to have Stephenson valve gear, arrives at Lightcliffe station, 7 July 1959. (GM)

Right:
No 44956 and No 44973 double-head an express passenger train leaving Arrochas on the West Highland line, 13 August 1960. The coaching stock is a mixture of standard BR Mk 1s (second and third coaches) and pre-nationalisation (first coach). (GM)

Left:
No 45100 fitted with a domed Short Firebox boiler hauls an express freight train on the Settle–Carlisle route at Horton in Ribblesdale, 23 May 1959. (GM)

Left:
No 44875 on a passenger train, 17 May 1952. The train is made up of pre-Grouping coaching stock. (GM)

Right:
No 45428 at Holbeck
shed, Leeds,
8 November 1967,
along with one of
the last 'Jubilee'
class locomotives
(No 45562 *Alberta*).
No 45428 is seen in
exceptionally clean
condition for 1967
as it had been
prepared as a
standby locomotive
for a Royal train
working carrying the
Duke of Edinburgh.
The royal household
had specified a
steam locomotive,
the train engine
being a 'Jubilee' also
from Holbeck. (GM)

Right:
No 45208 near Huddersfield in 1948/9 running under express passenger lamps but with a train of pre-Grouping coaching stock (possibly ex-LNWR). (AC)

Below:
No 45473 seen departing Kingmoor yard, Carlisle, 14 August 1960, with a fitted freight train. The locomotive is seen fitted with a riveted tender and tablet exchange apparatus. (GM)

Left:
No 45022 on an ordinary passenger train in Scotland, 30 October 1954. Note the route indicator just above the bufferbeam, a feature of Caledonian traffic working, and the unusual style and position of the cabside numerals. It has a domed boiler and riveted tender. (AC)

Below:
No 45109 double-headed at Watford, April 1957, with a 'Princess Royal' on the 'Merseyside Express' from Euston to Liverpool. (AC)

Above: No 44876 at Preston with the 21.23 hrs to Liverpool Exchange in 1967, almost at the end of steam. (CR/MAK)

DRAWINGS

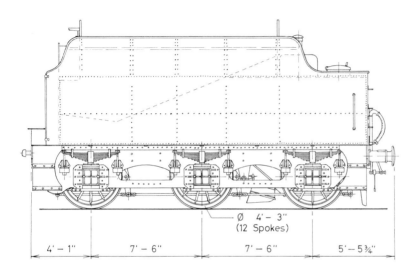

Ø 4' – 3"
(12 Spokes)

4' – 1"   7' – 6"   7' – 6"   5' – 5¾"

Alternative
Spring Hangers

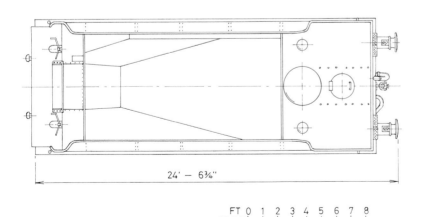

24' – 6¾"

FT 0 1 2 3 4 5 6 7 8
SCALE

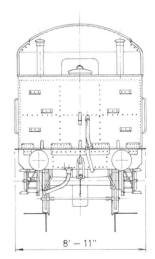

8' – 11"

Standard 4,000 gallon-tender (riveted)

© 2004 Railway Modeller/Ian Beattie.

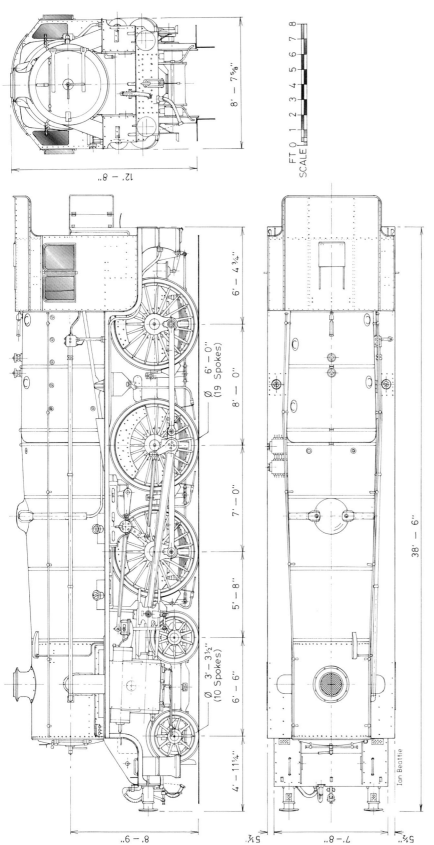

8' - 7⅝"

12' - 8"

FT 0 1 2 3 4 5 6 7 8
SCALE

6' - 4¾"

Ø 6' - 0"
(19 Spokes)

8' - 0"

7' - 0"

38' - 6"

5' - 8"

Ø 3' - 3½"
(10 Spokes)

6' - 6"

4' - 11¼"

8' - 9"

5¼"

7' - 8"

5¼"

Ian Beattie

Walschaerts valve gear

© 2004 Railway Modeller/Ian Beattie.

Below:
No 5157 *The Glasgow Highlander* in an official view taken in March 1936. Note the domeless Short Firebox boiler and the plain coupling rods on this Armstrong Whitworth-built locomotive. (LMS)

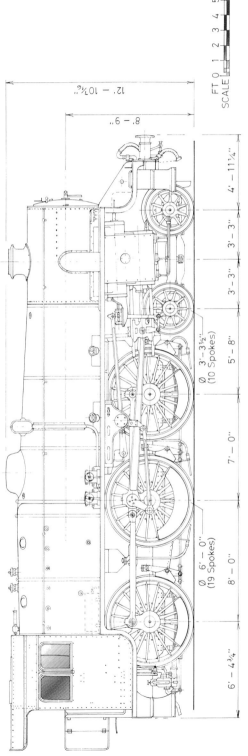

Walschaerts valve gear

© 2004 Railway Modeller/Ian Beattie.

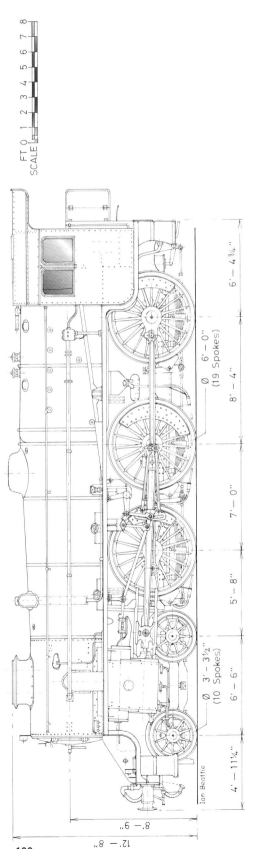

SCALE

FT 0 1 2 3 4 5 6 7 8

Ø 3' – 3½"
(10 Spokes)

4' – 11¼"

6' – 6"

Ø 6' – 0"
(19 Spokes)

5' – 8"

7' – 0"

8' – 4"

6' – 4¾"

8' – 9"

12' – 8"

Ian Beattie

No 4767 Stephenson valve gear

© 2004 Railway Modeller/Ian Beattie.

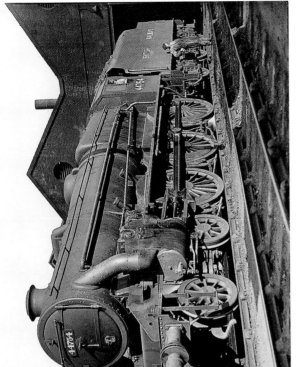

Above left:
No 44750 at Camden MPD on 11 May 1957. (CPB)

Above:
No 44754. The 20 Crewe-built locomotives had the cab cut-off at platform level. (PRW)

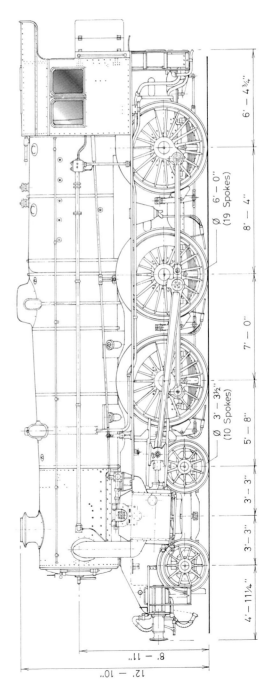

6' - 4¾"

Ø 6' - 0"
(19 Spokes)

8' - 4"

7' - 0"

Ø 3' - 3½"
(10 Spokes)

5' - 8"

3' - 3"

3' - 3"

4' - 11½"

8' - 11"

12' - 10"

1st series Caprotti locomotive

© 2004 Railway Modeller/Ian Beattie.

FT 0 1 2 3 4 5 6 7 8
SCALE

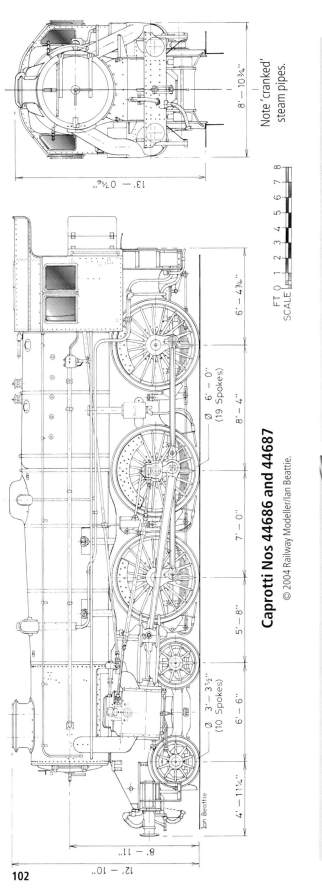

Note 'cranked' steam pipes.

13' - 0¹⁄₁₆"

8' - 10³⁄₄"

6' - 4³⁄₄"

Ø 6' - 0"
(19 Spokes)

8' - 4"

7' - 0"

5' - 8"

Ø 3' - 3¹⁄₂"
(10 Spokes)

6' - 6"

4' - 11¹⁄₄"

8' - 11"

12' - 10"

Ian Beattie

FT 0 1 2 3 4 5 6 7 8
SCALE

Caprotti Nos 44686 and 44687

© 2004 Railway Modeller/Ian Beattie.

Left:
Front three-quarter views of No 44686. Nos 44686 and 44687 were built at Horwich, and, as with the first series of Caprotti locomotives, had the cab cut-off at platform level. (RJH & BG)

Above:
No 44742 in purposeful pose at Llandudno. (IAL)

This page: No 45177 climbing Beattock on 1 August 1964. Note the electrification warning flashes and the change of position of the headlamp brackets on both the smokebox door and above the bufferbeam, this change was instigated during the spread of overhead electrification. (PR)